Resolution Invocation

Let this truly be
The celebration of
A New Year...
Let us remember
The past, yet
Not dwell in it.
Let us fully use
The present, yet
Not waste it.
Let us live for
The future, yet
Not count on it.
Let this truly be
The celebration of
A New Year,
As we remember
And appreciate
And live rejoicing
With each other.

Mattie J.T. Stepanek

Celebrate Through Heartsongs

Written and Illustrated by

Mattie J. T. Stepanek

Poet & Peacemaker

with a Foreword by Jerry Lewis

VSP Books

HYPERION

New York

This book is dedicated to my mom and
"grown-old" best friend, Jeni Stepanek, and to my
favorite adult best friend, Sandy Newcomb.
Thank you both for teaching me how to "celebrate life,
every day, in some way" through patience and
prayer and play.

ISBN: 0-7868-6945-3

Hyperion books are available for special promotions and premiums.
For details contact Hyperion Special Markets, 77 West 66th Street, 11th floor,
New York, New York, 10023, or call 212-456-0100.

FIRST EDITION

10 9 8 7 6 5 4 3 2 1

Foreword by Jerry Lewis

In my 71 years as an entertainer, I've been blessed to know many great people—from physicians to scientists to performers to world leaders—who had tremendous passion about what they did. When it comes to brilliance and accomplishment and creativity, I thought I'd pretty much seen it all. Then, sometime last year, I was given a book called *Heartsongs*, by a young person named Mattie Stepanek.

At first I was curious about Mattie's poetry because I knew he was affected by one of the diseases we at the Muscular Dystrophy Association are dedicated to defeating. When I began to read Mattie's words, I was stunned. They stirred feelings inside of me that I hadn't known existed. I found myself wondering, "Is this real? Can it be that a child of this age knows so much about love and life and spirituality?" Mattie's words had such magnificent depth and sensitivity that I felt they could only have come from a mind like that of Carl Sandburg or even Elie Wiesel. But then I read on and said to myself, "There has never been a mind quite like Mattie's."

The real joy was when I read some of the book with my 10-year-old daughter, Danielle. Mattie's poems are not just meant to be read, but to be shared.

I am so proud to have Mattie working alongside me as MDA National Goodwill Ambassador. He's such an illuminating force—I thank God every day for the passion he brings to this urgent mission, which is fully equal to the intensity he brings to his brilliant poetry. And that's saying a lot.

A new book by Mattie Stepanek is truly a cause for celebration. Let the celebration begin.

Jerry Lewis
National Chairman
Muscular Dystrophy Association

Acknowledgments

This book is about the celebration of life, through heartsongs. I want to thank many friends for helping me along my journey, which has too often had pebbles and boulders on the roads.

Thank you to the Beaudets for helping my mom and me start down a whole new path in our journey. Thank you to the Retzlaffs and Odens for being some of our human angels and making the journey so much easier. Thank you to the Moxes for opening their doors to us during a transition on the journey. Thank you to Oprah Winfrey and Jimmy Carter for supporting the spirit of hope and peace as we continue our journey. And, thank you to the Newcomb/Dobbins clan for *always* being there, with us and for us, in the celebration of our journey (even when it's difficult to find things to celebrate!).

Thank you to everyone at Children's National Medical Center, especially the people in the Pediatric ICU, the Pulmonary Department, and the Clown Care Unit, for continuing to provide the best medical care in the world so that many, many children can celebrate the gifts of life. A special thank you to Dr. Christi Corriveaux for asking me about my three wishes, to Marissa Garis for making sure they came true, and to Laura Becker for helping me to celebrate at home.

Thank you to everyone who supports the Muscular Dystrophy Association. Thank you to Jerry Lewis for celebrating the gifts of all children and adults with neuromuscular diseases. And thank you to all the people in the local Maryland, Virginia, and Washington, DC, offices and to those at the National Headquarters in Arizona for giving us gifts like MDA Summer Camp, and hope.

Thank you to people like Nell and Larry, Valerie, Mollie, Dr. Fink, Dr. Flotte, Katie, Gina, Cathy, Ann, Paula, and Tracey who have celebrated life with me for many years; to people like Dr. Fenton, Dr. Witzmann, Peggy, Terry, Mike, Bob, Mary Ellen, Camille, the Sullivans, and the Copelands who have more recently joined the celebration; and to Stephanie and Melissa for being my beautiful "co-wives."

Thank you to Most Holy Rosary, where "church" is truly "the people" who come together to celebrate. Thank you for the opportunities you've given me to grow spiritually and to share my gifts with others. Thank you to the choir for having fun while "making a joyful noise"; to Fr. Dixon for praying so hard for the world; to Megan, Maura, and Eileen for laughing with me; and, to Baby Katrina for always smiling at me.

Thank you to my brother Jamie, whose handprint is with the "Growing Up" poem in this book. My siblings, Jamie and Katie and Stevie, are always a part of my growing celebration of life.

And, as always, I say thank you to my mom, Jeni, who inspires me to play after every storm, to never give up the hope of every tomorrow, and to believe in the power of prayer for every today.

Love, Mattie

Contents

Celebrate Nature

How Poetry Grows

Be aware,
Be noticing,
Be inspired…
By something simple,
By something unusual,
By something that touches
Your mind or
Your spirit or
Your life.
Let the feeling move your heart,
Let the heart bring words to your mind,
Let the mind create a poem from your hand.
The poetry is then completed,
The poetry is then celebrated,
The poetry is then shared.
And so, other people will
Be aware,
Be noticing,
Be inspired….

January 2002

Rapture

Have you witnessed
The early morning?
Right before the
Sun rises, and
The sky glows
Purple lava-lamp?
The clouds are
The dark,
Floating
Lumps, and
The still
Gentle earth
Is to look upon.

December 2000

Nags Head Sunrise

The last two stars of the night,
The moon dimming into day,
Pink fingers of light reaching
Into less gray skies,
Dolphins playing in new waves,
Golden cloud-streaks greeting
The dawning ball of fire,
Up from the ocean...
Sunrise on the pier.

July 1998

4

The Importance of Colors

My favorite color
Used to be sunset
Because I love
Pink and orange and brown.
Now, I have
A second favorite color—
Rainbow.
A rainbow has all of my
Favorite sunset colors,
And also all the colors
That are in the sunrise
And in all the fish and birds
And in all the people
That God made.
Some of the kids at my school
Say that pink and orange
Are girls' colors.
But I don't think so
Because boys like
Sunsets too.
And I know that rainbows
Are for boys and girls,
Because they have
Pink and orange and brown
And gray and purple and blue.
I don't think
Girls and boys
Should have their own colors.
I think God wants us
To share colors,
And to like them all
Because they are all
A gift to us.

January 1995

5

Word Poetry I

From wild bouquets of
Morning wind and
Evening sound,
A song for all people
Blossoms and grows.

August 2001

RAIN

Rushing, pouring arrows of water,
Aiming towards the ground to feed earth,
In many different forms and seasons,
Nonstop until clouds tire and the sun wakes.

February 2000

Word Poetry V

Tell her why secret bouquets
Build only dry glass blossoms.
Let summer grow full, and teach
With windy lace, pronouncing songs
Sounding of page after book of life.

November 2001

About the Weeping Willow Tree

The weeping willow is such a sad, sad tree,
But it's also such a beautiful and graceful tree.
Weeping willows are probably sad
When they are remembering things.
Like maybe one of their brother or sister seeds
Grew into a tree that was cut down
One day or one year, and they don't know why.
Weeping willows are like people who are sad.
With drooping branches and leaves and woods.
Weeping willows are beautiful like people, too.
Beautiful like a rainbow-tree because of the shape.
Their branches bend and slide over and down.
Like rainbows that are sad because maybe
Someone got hurt during the storm
That came before the rainbow colors grew.
Weeping willow leaves are very small.
Like little Heaven-tears and wishing-leaves
That fall gently down from the sky to
The tree to the earth and the people.
Sometimes I am a weeping willow tree,
Especially when I don't understand
What I'm feeling or why things happen,
Like when people are mean or
Like when brothers and sisters die or
Like when God makes people with disabilities.
I don't like feeling like a weeping willow tree.
But sometimes, it's okay to feel that way, too.
Weeping willow trees are special and gentle,
And sometimes sad things are beautiful,
Just like sometimes happy things make us cry.

September 1996

7

Leaf Play

The cold wind blows,
And the leaves
Fall to the ground.
They have changed
Into beautiful colors.
On sunny days,
We can jump
In a pile of leaves,
But only if
We are wearing
Our play shoes.

October 1993

Magic-Leaves

I love the fall,
Because all of the leaves
Turn into colors.
Some turn into green...
They are my tree-leaves.
Some turn into brown...
They are my jungle leaves.
Some turn into orange...
They are my pumpkin leaves.
Some turn into yellow...
They are my butterfly-leaves.
Some turn into red...
They are my flower-leaves.
I love all of my colors.
They fall down to the ground,
So I can jump and play
And touch them,
It is magic.

October 1993

8

Winter Tops

When it's almost time for winter,
The dew on top of the grass turns to frost,
Your breath on top of the air turns to steam, and
A hat hides the hair on top of your head.
But when it's almost time for winter
And the clouds are a little bit late,
The trees, without any leaves on top,
Stand on their highest tippy-toes
And scratch-scratch-scratch at the sky.
Like a dog scratching on its owner's knees for a bone,
The winter-sticks are begging for snow.
Snow that will look beautiful and be fun for playing,
And snow that will feed the trees
So they can grow new tops after the winter.

December 1996

9

One Day

One day,
I will write a poem
About the
Giant snowflakes.
Such a beautiful sight
My eyes beheld during
Just any mid-morning.
Huge snowflakes,
The size of
Paper snowflakes
Little children cut out
To decorate
The winter season.
Enormous snowflakes,
Thick as pancakes,
But gently drifting
From the sky.

Magical snowflakes,
From an elsewhere space,
That transported me
To someplace
Where I traveled
Through a field of stars,
Frosting past me...
To me...
On me...
Yes, one day,
I will write a poem
About these
Amazing snowflakes,
As my Heartsong awakes.
Such a fantastic
White wonder
That led my mind
To wander,
One day.

February 2001

10

Between Winter and Summer

When the sun is in an empty sky
With not even one little cloud,
And the pink and white blossoms
Are winding from their trees
In a soft and warm breeze,
Then we know that the
Spring-King has come and the
Snow-King has gone for the year.
But the Spring-King is good
To the children and
To the grown-ups who play.
He gives us pink-blossom snow
To throw in the air and
To catch on our hands and
To smell in the spring sun
While we have the season
Between winter and summer.

April 1996

11

Butterfly Summer

This was a summer,
A Butterfly Summer.
A time and sign,
Of peace, grace, and
Happiness.
Beautiful rainbows of
So many colors, of
Rainbow butterflies.
This was a Summer,
A Butterfly Summer.

August 1998

Metaphor Lesson (I)

A bright blue sky
Is a cloak for the earth,
Keeping us cool, and
Yet keeping us warm.

April 2000

Metaphor Lesson (II)

A peaceful lake
Is a meditation
For the mind,
And for the spirit.

April 2000

Metaphor Lesson (VI)

In the evening,
The sun is
The precious gem
Of God's peace chain.

April 2000

Metaphor Lesson (XIII)

At night, the moon is
The marble eye of a
Curious rabbit, looking
Upon the world with interest.

April 2000

13

The Gift of Color

Thank You
For all the colors of the rainbow.
Thank You
For sharing these colors
With all of the fish
And all of the birds
And all of the flowers
That You have given us.
And Thank You
For the colors of the
Heaven-in-the-earth
And of the
Heaven-in-the-sky,
And for sharing these colors
In the people of the world.
You give us color
As a gift, God,
And I thank You
For all of these
Beautiful colors and
Beautiful things and
Beautiful people.
What special gifts
You have given to us!

January 1995

14

Celebrate
Thoughts and
Dreams

About Living (Part 1)

Life!
Something
To be celebrated...
Something
To be savored...
While it lasts.
For although
Life is wonderful,
Life is not forever.
People grow older,
And then they die.
Some people even die
Before they grow older.
Dying may seem
Sad and scary,
But once death is over,
We can actually Live
Forever in Heaven.

June 2000

17

Music for Life

Music is a part of life.
Like people, music
Comes in unique forms.
And, people like music
For many different reasons.
Mostly we like it
Because it touches
Our spirits
In some way,
Even if nothing else
Has touched our essence.
No matter what type
Of music we hear
On the outside,
It can awaken our
Heartsong on the inside.
And if we listen
To our Heartsongs
And bring them out,
We can have
A peaceful life,
A peaceful sense of self
And of family,
And be a part of
Creating a peaceful world.

February 2000

18

Peace of Color

A good, colorful world
Is the key to
A good, colorful life.
Remember that
Without color,
The world could
Be a dull place.
Listen to your
Heartsong
With color in
Your spirit.
Then, you will be
A part of the
Harmony and peace
Kaleidoscope
That reflects
Our changing world.

January 2000

19

About Heaven...

Now, I will tell you about Heaven.
Where is Heaven?
It is way over there, and
It is way over there, and
It is way over there, too.
It is Everywhere.
What does it look like?
It looks like a school, and
It looks like a farm, and
It looks like a home.
It looks like Everything.
What does it sound like?
Well,
I really don't know,
Because I am just
A little big boy
With a brother,
And another brother and sister,
And a friend,
Who live in the
Everywhere and Everything of Heaven.
But perhaps,
Heaven sounds like
Forever.

May 1994

Post-Terrorism Haiku

Let us remember...
We are the land of the free,
Not of the vengeful.

Let us remember...
It is in God that we trust,
Not in bombs and guns.

Let us remember...
Peace grows from a gentle heart,
Not one filled with spite.

September 2001

Hope Haiku

Gentle, and peaceful...
We are the children of one God,
Yet, so many faiths.

True, we are different...
Unique mosaic of life,
Still, we are the same.

United, we are...
The festive fabric of life.
Divided, we fall.

September 2001

22

Simple Ablution

Sometimes,
People complain that
Others cry too much.
How sad.
How angering.
How blundering.
Tears are like rain.
They come
Gently, or strongly.
They come
Quietly, or loudly.
They come
Refreshingly, or devastatingly.
But they always,
In some way, come,
And cleanse, and console.
Sometimes,
There's a mess to fix
After the rain,
After the tears,
But it always makes people
Stop.
And think.
And take notice.

Perhaps,
We should all cry
More.
Together.
For each other.
Perhaps,
If everyone in the world
Cried with and for
Other people and life,
We might be
More caring and peaceful.
Perhaps,
We could cry enough
That the world would be
A cleaner and healthier place,
For our people,
For our life,
For our future.

December 2001

23

About Meanings

When
Life is good,
It means
You are
Growing up.
And when
You are
Growing up,
It means
Life is good.

February 2000

24

About Things That Matter

It matters that the world knows
We must celebrate the gift of life
Every day in some way, and
We must always remember
To play after every storm.
It matters that the world knows
All children are truly blessed
With the innocent gifts of gentleness,
Trust, and compassion, which
Should guide the wisdom of
   grown-ups.
It matters that the world knows
We each have a song in our heart
That can inspire us in good times and
Hard times if we take the time to listen.
It matters that the world knows
Our senses can help us discover
The hidden and non-hidden
Enchantment in life, if we use them
   fully.
It matters that the world knows
We must choose our words and wants
Carefully, or we could forever hurt
   others
With these most dangerous weapons.

It matters that the world knows
Strength and value of all things
   created
Must be measured by character
   and commitment
Rather than by might and wealth.
It matters that the world knows
We must heed the valuable lessons of
Everyday life, through the celebration of
Children and Heartsongs, senses
   and words,
Or we could lose in our journey
   to the future.
It matters that the world knows
A person by my name and being existed
With a strong spirit and an eternal
   mindset
To become a peacemaker for all,
By sharing the things that really
   matter.

June 2001

25

About Memories

Memories are a great gift.
Memories are given to us by God,
As a keepsake and a treasure.
Memories allow us to call upon the past
Without reliving it.
Memories offer us opportunities
To laugh, or to cry,
To smile, or to reminisce
About old events and experiences.
Memories help us
Learn about the past,
So that we can pass on
Great happenings to young learners.
Memories support us
As we cautiously step into our future.
Memories teach us
About what things are good to repeat.
Memories warn us
About what things should never
Be allowed to happen again.
If we open our minds,
Memories allow and offer
And help and support
And teach and warn
About life.
Memories are a gift of the past,
That we hold in the present,
To create what can be a great future.
Treasure and keep memories,
For the sake of Life.

June 2000

Celebrate
Special Days

First Day

Fireworks in my head and stomach,
Not knowing what I'll find or do next.
Hopefully, I will get used to it,
Let it become a new part
Of my exciting, everyday life.

September 1999

A Birthday Card

Happy Birthday, Jamie!
God is blessing you—
Right now,
And all day
And all night,
And all life.
Even though you died,
You are all-life, Jamie.
With your wisdom,
You can share your spirit with me,
And come into my heart.
You can give me wisdom, too,
So I can be a good boy forever.
And when I die,
I will go to Heaven,
And I will be so happy to see you again,
And we will be together
With all-life Forever.
Even though your
Body doesn't live with us anymore,
You are still-and-always my brother.
I love you forever, Jamie,
From your little brother, Mattie.
Happy Birthday!

February 1996

Sound of Rain

Angels' footsteps
Gently dancing
From the Heavens.
Tiny drop-prints
Of wetness touch
Around the earth,
Reminding us of
Important things,
Like Jesus washing
The Apostles' feet.

January 1998

About Easter-time

Easter is a long time away.
It comes when
The rains come,
Because that is when
New things grow,
And we have
New life,
Just like in Heaven.

November 1994

Memorial Day

This is a holiday
That means we are free.
We can run and play.
We can have food and friends,
Because the soldier
Made our country free.
I like living in
The United States of America,
And in Maryland.
And because this is a holiday,
That means we are free
And should go to the donut store.

May 1994

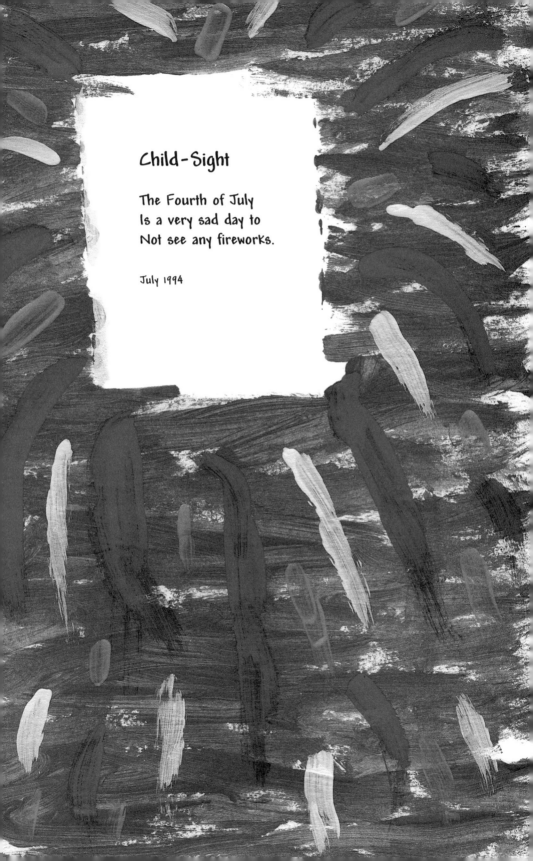

Child-Sight

The Fourth of July
Is a very sad day to
Not see any fireworks.

July 1994

Metaphor Lesson (IX)

A vacation
Is a three-to-ten-day nap
In the middle
Of a busy season.

April 2000

Nags Head Sunset

The sunset is very beautiful
In Nags Head.
It reflects off the water,
Orange and yellow and
Gold come from the sky
To the sound and the ocean.
The colors come to the people,
To make us feel happy.
I feel a lot of things.
Mostly, I feel relaxed.

August 1997

On Being Prepared

This year for Halloween
I think I might want to be a
Warlock-witch again.
Or maybe Cornelius, the Prince.
Or a skeleton,
Yeah, a skeleton.
Or maybe Santa.
Or the Grinch-Santa!
Or maybe Captain Hook,
Or a dinosaur,
Or a fish,
Or a tree.
Maybe I'll be a clown,
Or a bunny,
Or a monkey,
Or a bumblebee.
Or I could be Peter Pan.
Oh, or maybe an Angel,
Or the Good Shepherd,
Or a lamb.
Or I could be Pinocchio again.
Or, well,
Mommy, have you noticed
That I want to be
All of those things?
And maybe,
I won't be any of them,
But something different.
Gosh!
That's a lot of costumes
And a lot of deciding to do.
And it's only March!

March 1994

35

October

The candlelight flickers more
And more, and even the house
Seems to tremble in the chilly air.
The days grow short as a
Black cat, and the light becomes
Darker, like blue-violet.
The flower petals bloom to the
Ground, and the stems wither
Into crackling leaves, then
Under the dirt, like pigs
Covered in mud for protection.
The spiders are nesting together
Looking for warm places to web.
Seeing them sends shivers
Down your spine, and
Reminds you that the
Creepy-crawlies in your head,
Howling and whispering "BOO!"
Are getting ready for Halloween.
And then, you smell the
Sweetness of pumpkin pie, and
Candy corn in the fresh air of fall,
And you remember that
October brings a season of
Feelings and excitement.

October 1997

King James and the Sad Pilgrim

On Thursday,
It will be Thanksgiving Day.
I learned about
King James and the Pilgrims
At my school.
I drew pictures of them.
King James looks
Silly and confused.
The Pilgrim looks sad.
I'm not sure why
He is so sad,
But I think it's maybe
Because he is
Not in the same land as his King
Anymore.
But even though
They aren't together,
The Pilgrim will have a Feast
And try to be happy
With the other Pilgrims.
He will say,
"I am thankful for this food,
And for rainbows and feathers
And sunsets and sunrises,
And for my family and my life,
And especially,
For Angels."

November 1994

About the Spirit

Some people think Christmas
Comes from a box or a store...
But they are wrong.
Christmas comes from the heart.
It is the Spirit of Santa Claus.
Some people think Santa Claus
Is a man in red who gives us lots
And lots of what-we-choose gifts...
But they are wrong.
Santa comes from the heart.
He is the Spirit of Christmas.
Joy and happiness and love
And the celebrations of life
All come from the Spirit.
Some people believe these truths...
But some people do not have faith.
I believe in the Spirit of Christmas.
And I believe in the Spirit of Santa,
They both come from the heart, and
They are real because we believe...
And we are the Spirit of the Season.

November 1998

Happy Holydays

True courage
Is when we find
Bravery
In the midst of
Fear.
Each year,
Let us celebrate
The holidays
With the spirit of tradition,
Decorating in greens and golds
And Santa-suit colors.
But this year,
Let us also honor
The holidays
With the spirit of courage,
Remembering in colors
That echo of heroism...
Reds, and whites, and blues.

December 2001

Resolution Invocation

Let this truly be
The celebration of
A New Year....
Let us remember
The past, yet
Not dwell in it.
Let us fully use
The present, yet
Not waste it.
Let us live for
The future, yet
Not count on it.
Let this truly be
The celebration of
A New Year,
As we remember
And appreciate
And live rejoicing
With each other.

January 2002

Gentle Blessings

God Bless Katie...
God Bless Stevie...
God Bless Jamie...
And God Bless the Christmas Tree.

December 1992

Celebrate Life

Celebrate the World

We had cake at school today.
It was a celebration,
But it wasn't anybody's birthday.
It was a celebration
Of the world.
The world needs a birthday celebration.
The world has lots and lots of friends,
And I am one of the world's friends,
So I celebrated today.
I said thank you to the world,
And thank You to God for the world,
And also,
Thank you for the cake
That made it a celebration of life!

July 1994

45

In Whom We Can Trust...

Of God, the world is made:
Sky and water, and earth...
Sticks and stones.
Of dust, all life is made:
Plants and animals, and people...
Feelings and free will.
Of people, problems are made:
Within the self and the family,
And within all nations...
Between the nations.
To survive, to thrive,
Some are blessed with
A person to trust...
A parent, a social worker, a judge,
To guide us in growing,
To support us in coping,
To help us in mediating.
But in whom can each of us
Always have trust?
In God we can trust, and because
We are made in God's image...
Wise and loving, and powerful,
If we believe,
We can trust in ourselves,
And make a peaceful difference...
In the world, and in life.

May 2000

46

Not Quite What I Expected

It's the last day of school!
Everyone is so happy!
They're laughing,
Running around, and
Talking with friends.
I expected that!
I expected happy kids, and
I expected sad teachers,
Who would miss their students.
I went out with the teachers
To wave goodbye to the buses
Loaded with cheering kids.
The teachers waved,
So sadly, and shouted:
"Bye! Miss you! Be good!
Have a nice summer!"
Then, when the last bus
Was out of sight,
Mrs. Jenkins went out
On the blacktop and
Danced around singing,
"Hooray! They're gone!
We're free! We're free!"
All the other teachers
Laughed and clapped.
Sometimes, things are
Not quite what I expected.

June 1998

As It Was in the Beginning

When the playground is
Roaring with kids...
When the sky is
Thundering with sunshine...
When the atmosphere is
Electrified with glee...
Then is when we know
For sure that life is
Thriving...
Reverberating...
Exhilarating...
It is good, indeed.

June 2000

Children at Heart

My mom and I
Will always be
Children at heart.
We will always cherish
The magic of imagination.
The excitement of adventure,
And, the importance of playing.
My mom and I
Will always be
Children at heart...
For we know how
To celebrate life!

July 2000

MDA Summer Camp Is

MDA Summer Camp is
...A place where kids wish
Onto paper that is placed into
Balloon-carried baskets,
Then hopefully pray as
Their thoughts and dreams
Ascend into the heavens.
MDA Summer Camp is
...A feeling of friends
Helping friends,
Whoever they are,
However they are,
Wherever they are,
For whatever reason,
Just because they are.
MDA Summer Camp is
...An understanding
That the worth of a person
Should never be measured
By number of years lived, or
By physical or mental abilities,
But by the strength of spirit.
MDA Summer Camp is
...A time for commemoration,
And liberation,
And rejuvenation,
And celebration,
In spite of the realities of life.
...Thank God, that
MDA Summer Camp IS.

Summer 2000

MDA—Muscular Dystrophy Association

About Living (Part II)

Although I am
Greatly anticipating
Going to Heaven
When I die,
I would really like
To finish my life
On earth as a mortal
For a long time first.
But,
I know that life
On earth is limited.
And,
I know that Life
In Heaven is eternal.
So,
Every day,
No matter who we are,
What we do, or
Where we are,
We must celebrate
The gift of life on earth
While we have it,
For Ever.

June 2000

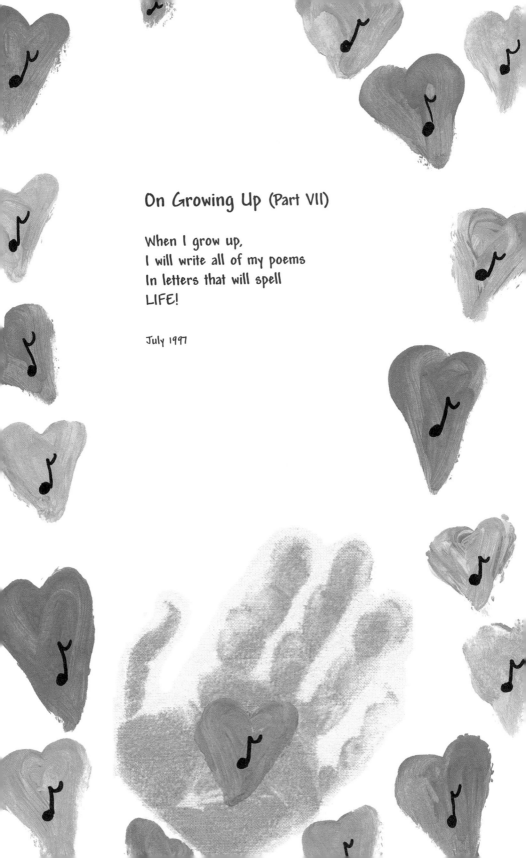

On Growing Up (Part VII)

When I grow up,
I will write all of my poems
In letters that will spell
LIFE!

July 1997

Eternal Role Call

I will paint rainbows
When the spring comes,
And children will dance
And smile in the music of my colors.
I will shape clouds
When the summer comes,
And children will chant
And dream in the melody of my creations.
I will whistle winds
When the fall comes,
And children will listen
And hum in the understanding of leaves.
I will jingle stars
When the winter comes,
And children will laugh
And believe in the ballads of the season.
I will revolve seasonally
When my death comes,
And children will remember
And share their Heartsongs,
Celebrating the gifts in the circle of life.

January 2002

Celebrate
Everyday Heroes

Special and Beautiful People

Look how God made me!
Look at my special smile!
Everyone is special,
With different smiles,
And different skins.
We are all like
Beautiful flowers.
Like beautiful rainbows
And feathers
That fall so gentle
Onto our hands.
Just look at us!
God made us so special!
We are beautiful people,
And we should
Share our smiles
All of the time!

January 1995

School Nurse

Sometimes,
I think Mrs. Rich is an angel in disguise.
Really, I do.
She is like an angel with
Invisible wings and halo,
So gentle and caring and good.
She is always helpful and
Nice to other people, even
When everything is frustrating
All around her, and the world.
Sometimes,
I think Mrs. Rich is an angel in disguise,
And I am thankful
That I am one of the lucky ones
Who gets touched and hugged
By such a special spirit.

June 1999

56

On Being a King

When Grandmaster Lee was
A little boy, like me,
He wanted to be a king!
A king must be good.
He cannot be mean and nasty.
A king must be respectful and
A king must be loving.
Well, sometimes people can
Be like a king, but not
Really like a king in stories.
Grandmaster Lee grew up into a man
And he is not a king,
But he is a teacher, like the Lord.
He is respectful and loving,
And he is not mean and nasty.
He is very, very good.
He is a "real life" hero
Just like God is the hero in my heart.
And even though Grandmaster Lee
Grew up and never got to be a king,
He is like a king to me.
He told me that even though bodies die,
A good heart lives forever.
I might grow up.
I want to grow up.
Grandmaster Lee says I will grow up, too.
And when I grow up,
I will be respectful and loving,
Just like my teacher, Grandmaster Lee...
My King of Hapkido.

November 1995

57

About Court—According to Judge Woods

Q1. What do judges look for?

A. The truth.

Q2. Can judges tell who is truthful?

A. Mostly, yes.

Q3. Where might I talk with the judge?

A. In the judge's chamber.

Q4. Will age 7 1/2 be required in the courtroom?

A. Usually, no.

Q5. What do judges wear?

A. A long blue robe. (I got to try one on!)

Q6. Who takes notes?

A. The court recorder using a special machine.

Q7. Who protects the judge
and keeps order in the courthouse?

A The sheriff.

Q8. How do judges know who tells the truth?

A. They look into their eyes and faces
and listen to their hearts and words.

Q9. Where do judges sit?

A. In a big chair, at a big desk, with a big
computer, in the front of the courtroom.

Q10. What do judges do when they're bored?

A. They play computer solitaire games.

April 1998

58

Game Check

It is a chess game,
And I am in check.
I am not in Check-Mate,
Just a very tricky check.
I do not know the
Right moves, because
I am only a kid,
Just learning this game.
Dangerous, but not exciting.
Pieces get threatened and
Pieces can get captured.
But I have a good Queen.
She has power, and
She can keep me
Out of Check-Mate,
Even when he whispers, "Check!"
It is a tricky situation.
There are many moves ahead.
But my Queen is strong.
She will protect me.
His Queen has power, too,
But my Queen sees her moves,
And she will not let me go down.

October 1998

Samantha's Song

At the North Pole today,
The little girl who
Loves holding hands
Was not there.
I learned
She is in Heaven now.
The little girl who
Loves the gift of touch
Is holding God's hand.

December 2000

For Neil

Sometimes,
Red and yellow
Make me think of the sun,
As it rises and sets,
And shines for the passing of time.
Sometimes,
Red and yellow
Make me think of choice apples,
Delicious and juicy,
And baked into pies and delights.
Sometimes,
Red and yellow
Make me think of autumn tree stars,
As they dance and swirl
And crisp the flavor of this season.
But most of the times,
Red and yellow
Make me think of my friend,
Clapping and smiling
As he waits for summer camp,
And believes in the
Happiness of favorite colors.

December 2001

Every Little Star

Every little star,
Every shining star,
Every single night
When we look outside,
We can see
Little shining stars—
And then we know.
We know we can sing to Jamie,
And we sing:
    Shine little stars,
    Shine up in the sky.
    Twinkle, twinkle little stars,
    Shine and twinkle all
    Around my brother, Jamie.
    Shine and twinkle all
    Around the Heaven in the sky,
    Twinkle and shine,
    Every little star,
    Every little star,
    For my special, special Jamie.
    For my special, special brother.

June 1994

All About Friends

You can have more than one friend,
Even if you have a favorite best friend.
Friends are all different.
They come in many
Sizes, colors, ages, and abilities.
Friends are like rainbows,
Heartsongs, and life...
They are a gift from God.

January 1997

Created Bonds

Just like real family,
Kin help us to live
Our lives peacefully.
And we help them to live
Peacefully in return,
Because we are
Family and kin, together.
It is good to have family.
It is even better to have kinship
Within and beyond family.
For it is not blood
That creates a bond...
It is the unique
Relationship of mutual
Goals of love, and
Our celebration of life.

May 2000

62

About Fathers

A father is someone who
Takes you fishing and camping,
Makes you ice cream treats
   and malts,
Gets out your tickle stones,
Plays games and watches movies
   with you,
Gives you special surprises and
   puzzles,
And even howls with you under
   the full moon.
A father is someone who
Makes sure you have a safe
   place to live,
Shares prayer and good food
   with you,
Tells you when you've done
   good and
Corrects you when you need it,
Cares for you when you're sick,
Adapts things for you when
   you have a disability,
Teaches you science and math
   and respect
And even how to drive a tractor.

A father is someone who
Is sometimes called Dad
   or Daddy,
But also Uncle Paw,
   and Uncle Don,
And Mr. Mike, and Papa,
   and Vito,
And even Mom, sometimes.
A father is someone who
Encourages you to grow and be,
Talks with you about important
   things,
Listens to you about little things,
Lets you know you matter in
   the world,
And truly loves you like a son,
Even if you're only related by life.

December 1999

My Mommy

Graceful blue,
Loving pink,
Joyful yellow...
I rejoice to be
Cared for by this
Rainbow flower.

November 1999

An Angel Through My Mommy

My Mommy comes through
In many different ways...
She sees through
The eyes of an Angel,
With which everything and
Everyone is somehow beautiful.
She feels through
The touch of an Angel,
And knows which
Touches are good or bad.
She helps through
The care of an Angel,
Being there for me in my life,
And for every friend and kin.
She acts through
The spirit of an Angel,
Knowing when to comfort and
When to laugh and to cry.
My Mommy comes through
In many different ways...
And in all of them,
The world is blessed through
The life of an Angel...
My Mommy.

May 2000

65

Metaphor Lesson (VIII)

A smiling baby
Is a welcome sign,
Inviting others
Into a gentle world.

April 2000

Political Correctness

When I grow up,
People may ask me
If I would please
Give their babies a kiss.
And, if they don't,
I will ask the people
If I please may!

June 2001

66

The "ME" Poem

Magic of Heartsongs,
Afraid of a memory and the dark,
Truthful and sincere,
Teacher of peace,
Inspiring, intelligent, lover of ice cream,
Enthusiastic and ebullient.

Sunset watcher, shell and rock collector,
Tiger in Martial Arts,
Excited about celebrating life,
Playful, prayerful, patient,
Always ready with a hug and smile,
Never at a loss for words,
Energetic (like the Energizer Bunny)
Keeps on reading and writing
      and reading and writing...
        This is ME!

March 1998

I AM

I am black.
I am white.
I am all skins in between.
I am young.
I am old.
I am each age that has been.
I am scrawny.
I am well-fed.
I am starving for attention.
I am famous.
I am cryptic.
I am hardly worth the mention.
I am short.
I am height.
I am any frame or stature.
I am smart.
I am challenged.
I am striving for a future.

I am able.
I am weak.
I am some strength, I am none.
I am being.
I am thought.
I am all things, said and done.
I am born.
I am died.
I am dust of humble roots.
I am grace.
I am pain.
I am labor of willed fruits.
I am slave.
I am free.
I am bonded to my life.
I am rich.
I am poor.
I am wealth amid strife.

I am shadow.
I am glory.
I am hiding from my shame.
I am hero.
I am loser.
I am yearning for a name.
I am empty.
I am proud.
I am seeking my tomorrow.
I am growing.
I am fading.
I am hope amid the sorrow.
I am certain.
I am doubtful.
I am desperate for solutions.
I am leader.
I am student.
I am fate and evolutions.

I am spirit.
I am voice.
I am memory, not recalled.
I am chance.
I am cause.
I am effort, blocked and walled.
I am hymn.
I am heard.
I am reasoned without rhymes.
I am past.
I am nearing.
I am present in all times.
I am many.
I am no one.
I am seasoned by each being.
I am me.
I am you.
I am all-souls now decreeing
...I AM.

February 2001

69

Shades of Life

The color of sky
Is blues and grays.
The color of earth
Is greens and browns.
The color of hope
Is rainbows and purple.
And the color of peace
Is people, together.

January 2002

Index